My Book of Birds

Formerly titled
THE PARROT BOOK

By Tibor Gergely

MERRIGOLD PRESS • NEW YORK

Macaws
are large,
noisy members
of the
parrot
family.

They have feathers of many colors.

This big, beautiful bird
is a parrot.

Parrots that live with people
sometimes learn to talk.

Cockatoos are parrots, too.

They live for many years.

Parakeets are tiny parrots.

They come in
many colors.

The peacock is one

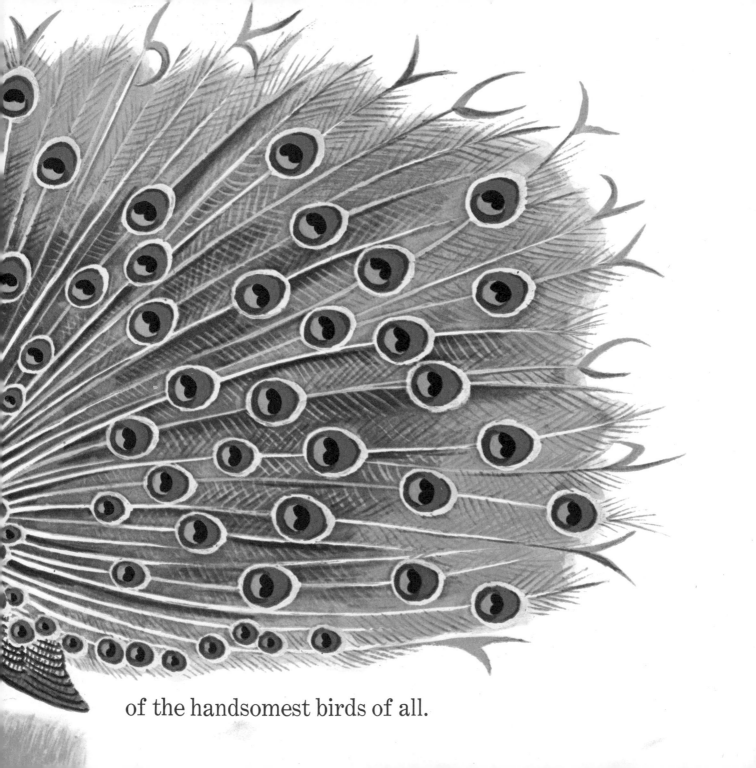

of the handsomest birds of all.

Toucans' bills
are almost bigger
than their bodies.

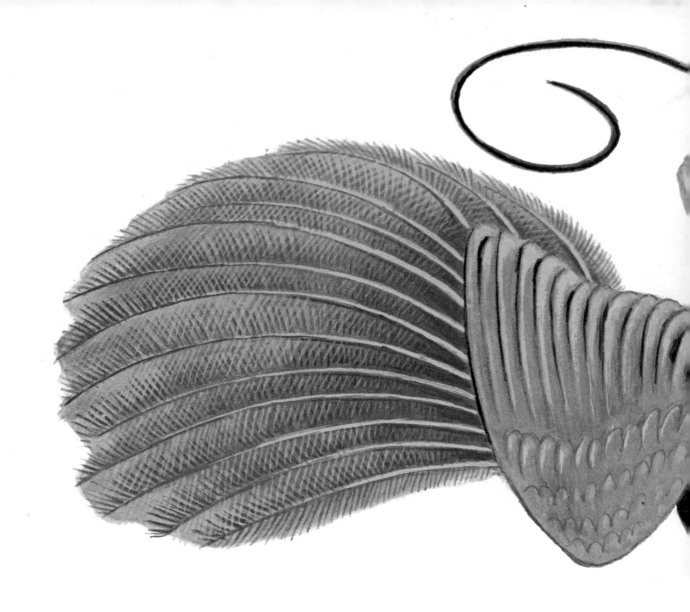

This is an upside-down bird-of-paradise.

He is showing off for his mate.

The baby wood ducks are learning
to swim with their mother.
The mandarin duck is watching them.

Both brown and white pelicans can hold many fish in the pouches under their bills.

Bright-colored flamingos dip their beaks underwater to get food.

During the time when they nest, flamingos live in large flocks.

Pretty little canaries are fine singers.
People often keep canaries as pets.

When the baby penguin grows up,
he will be black and white
like his parents.